1 2 3

JUGGLE WITH ME!

A COUNTING BOOK

by
Ilse-Margret Vogel

gb

GOLDEN PRESS • Western Publishing Company, Inc.
Racine, Wisconsin

Fourth Printing, 1974

© 1970 by Western Publishing Company, Inc.
GOLDEN, A LITTLE GOLDEN BOOK®, and GOLDEN PRESS®
are trademarks of Western Publishing Company, Inc.

I can juggle 1 ball
And it does not fall!

Is that all?
Just one ball?

I can do
Much better than you!

Look! I juggle 2

You mean juggling two
Is all you can do?

It's one, two, **3**

When I juggle, you see.

One, two, three—

That's nothing for me!

Look, look! I juggle 4

Four are not many.
I can do more.

Juggling 5
  Is easy for me.
I keep four in the air
  And bounce one on my knee.

You juggle five
   It's amazing to see
Four fly through the air
   And one bounce on your knee.

You can't juggle six?
That isn't so good.
You should have tried to—
Really, you should.

7 are almost too many for me,
Yet I manage to keep them all going, you see.

He keeps seven going.
Can you do more?
If you try hard,
You might beat his score.

I can almost do 8 –
Almost, but not quite.
One ball always falls.
I can't do it right.

Eight are too many?
I really don't see
How such a thing
Could possibly be.

I think it's great
To juggle eight!

I even feel fine
When I juggle 9

Nine are just fine,
But what about ten?
Who in the world
Can juggle ten?

YOU can juggle ten.

When you all play together,

You can juggle 10!

Yes, I will say it
Over again.
When you all play together,
You CAN juggle ten!